"E̶ ̶F̶R̶O̶M̶ ̶ DROWNED PEOPLE..."

BOOKS
EDINBURGH

PRIMO LEVI
Born 1919, Turin, Italy
Died 1987, Turin, Italy

All poems are taken from *Collected Poems*,
first published in 1988.

LEVI IN PENGUIN MODERN CLASSICS
A Tranquil Star
If Not Now, When?
The Complete Works of Primo Levi
The Periodic Table
Moments of Reprieve

PRIMO LEVI

The Survivor

Translated by Jonathan Galassi

PENGUIN BOOKS

PENGUIN CLASSICS

UK | USA | Canada | Ireland | Australia
India | New Zealand | South Africa

Penguin Books is part of the Penguin Random House group
of companies whose addresses can be found at
global.penguinrandomhouse.com.

All poems taken from *Collected Poems*, first published 1988
This selection first published 2018
001

Set in 11.6/15 pt Dante MT Std
Typeset by Jouve (UK), Milton Keynes
Printed in Great Britain by Clays Ltd, St Ives plc

ISBN: 978-0-241-33941-1

www.greenpenguin.co.uk

MIX
Paper from
responsible sources
FSC® C018179

Penguin Random House is committed to a
sustainable future for our business, our readers
and our planet. This book is made from Forest
Stewardship Council® certified paper.

Contents

Buna*

Wounded feet and cursed earth,
The line long in the gray mornings.
Buna's thousand chimneys smoke,
A day like every other day awaits us.
The sirens are terrific in the dawn:
'You, multitude with wasted faces,
Another day of suffering begins
On the monotonous horror of the mud.'

I see you in my heart, exhausted comrade;
Suffering comrade, I can read your eyes.
In your breast you have cold hunger nothing
The last courage has been broken in you.
Gray companion, you were a strong man,
A woman traveled next to you.
Empty comrade who has no more name,
A desert who has no more tears,

* The name of the factory where I worked while
I was a prisoner.

So poor that you have no more pain,
So exhausted you have no more fear,
Spent man who was a strong man once:
If we were to meet again
Up in the sweet world under the sun,
With what face would we confront each other?

December 28, 1945

Singing[*]

. . . But then when we began to sing
Those good old silly songs of ours,
It was as if everything
Was still the way it used to be.

A day was nothing but a day:
And seven of them make a week.
Killing was something wrong to us;
Dying, something far away.

And the months pass rather fast,
But there are still so many left!
We were merely young again:
Not martyrs, infamous, or saints.

This and much else came to mind
While we kept on singing;
But they were things like clouds,
And not easy to explain.

January 3, 1946

[*] Cf. Siegfried Sassoon, 'Everyone sang.'

February 25, 1944[*]

I'd like to believe something beyond,
Beyond death destroyed you.
I'd like to be able to say the fierceness
With which we wanted then,
We who were already drowned,
To be able someday to walk again together
Free under the sun.

January 9, 1946

* Cf. *Inferno* III:57, *Purgatory* V:134, and T. S. Eliot,
The Waste Land: 'I had not thought death had undone
so many.'

Song of the Crow I

'I've come from very far away
To bring bad news.
I crossed the mountain,
I flew through the low cloud,
I saw my belly mirrored in the pond.
I flew without rest,
A hundred miles without rest,
To find your window,
To find your ear,
To bring you the sad news
To take the joy from your sleep,
To spoil your bread and wine,
To sit in your heart each evening.'
   So he sang obscenely dancing
   Outside the window, on the snow.
   When he stopped, he stared malevolent,
   Etched a cross on the ground with his beak,
   And spread his black wings.

January 9, 1946

Shemà*

You who live safe
In your heated houses
You who come home at night to find
Hot food and friendly faces:

Consider if this is a man,
Who toils in the mud
Who knows no peace
Who fights for half a loaf
Who dies by a yes or a no.
Consider if this is a woman,
With no hair and no name
With no more strength to remember
With empty eyes and a womb as cold
As a frog in winter.

* Shemà means 'Hear' in Hebrew. It is the first word
of the basic prayer of Judaism, which affirms the unity
of God. Some lines of this poem paraphrase it.

Ponder that this happened:
I consign these words to you.
Carve them into your hearts
At home or on the street,
Going to bed or rising:
Tell them to your children.
Or may your house fall down,
May illness make you helpless,
And your children turn their eyes from you.

January 10, 1946

Get Up*

In the savage nights we dreamed
Dense and violent dreams
Dreamed with soul and body:
Of returning; eating; telling.
Until the dawn command
Resounded curt and low:
　　　'Wstawać';
And our hearts broke in our breasts.

Now we're home again.
Our bellies are full,
We've finished telling.
It's time. Soon we'll hear again
The strange command:
　　　'Wstawać.'

January 11, 1946

* *Wstawać* means 'get up' in Polish.

Monday

What is sadder than a train?
That leaves on time,
That only makes one sound,
That only goes one way.
Nothing's sadder than a train.

Unless it is a cart horse.
It's locked between two poles.
It can't even look askance.
Its whole life is plodding.

And a man? Isn't a man sad?
If he lives alone for long
If he thinks time is over,
A man's a sad thing, too.

January 17, 1946

After R. M. Rilke*

Lord, it is time: the wine's fermenting now.
The time has come to have a house,
Or to go without one a long time.
The time has come to not be alone,
Or we'll live alone for a long time:
We'll spend the hours at our books,
Or writing letters to far away,
Long letters from our solitude;
And we'll pace up and down the avenues,
Restless, while the leaves fall.

January 29, 1946

* Cf. 'Herbsttag,' from *Das Buch der Bilder*.

Sunset at Fòssoli*

I know what it means not to come back.
Through barbed wire I've seen
The sun go down and die.
I've felt the old poet's words
Tear at my flesh:
'Suns can set and rise again:
For us, once our brief light is spent,
There's one endless night to sleep.'

February 7, 1946

* Cf. Catullus, V, 4. Fòssoli, near Carpi, was the site of
the transit camp for prisoners bound for deportation.

February 11, 1946

I looked for you in the stars
When as a child I questioned them.
I asked the mountains for you
But all they gave me were a few moments
of solitude and short-lived peace.
Since you weren't there, those long evenings
I contemplated the mad blasphemy
That the world was one of God's mistakes,
And I was one of the world's.
But when, in the face of death,
I shouted no with every fiber,
That I wasn't through,
That I still had too much to do,
It was because you were there in front of me,
You with me beside you, as today,
A man a woman under the sun.
I came back because you were there.

February 11, 1946

The Glacier

We stopped, and dared to look
Into the grieving green jaws below,
And the courage in our hearts went slack
As happens when one loses hope.
A sad power sleeps in him;
And when, in the silence of the moon,
At night he sometimes screams and roars,
It's because, torpid giant dreamer that he is,
He's trying to turn over but cannot
In his bed of stone.

Avigliana, March 15, 1946

13

The Witch

A long time under the covers
She hugged the wax to her breast
Until it was soft and warm.
Then she got up, and gently, carefully,
With a loving patient hand
Molded the living effigy
Of the man who was in her heart.
When she was done, she threw oak
And grape and olive leaves on the fire
With his image, so it would melt.

She felt she was dying from the pain
Because the charm had worked,
And only then could she cry.

Avigliana, March 23, 1946

Wait

This is the time of lightning without thunder,
This is the time of unheard voices,
Restless sleep and pointless sleeplessness.
Comrade, let's not forget the days
Of long easy silences,
Of friendly streets at night,
And calm contemplation,
Before the leaves fall,
Before the sky shuts down again,
Before the familiar clang of iron feet
Rouses us again
Outside our doors.

January 2, 1949

Song of the Crow II*

'What is the number of your days? I've counted
    them:
Few and brief, and each one heavy with cares;
With anguish about the inevitable night,
When nothing saves you from yourself;
With fear of the dawn that follows,
With waiting for me, who wait for you,
With me who (hopeless, hopeless to escape!)
Will chase you to the ends of the earth,
Riding your horse,
Darkening the bridge of your ship
With my little black shadow,
Sitting at the table where you sit,
Certain guest at every haven,
Sure companion of your every rest.

* Cf. T. S. Eliot, *The Hollow Men*: 'This is the way the
world ends / Not with a bang but a whimper.'

'Till what was prophesied has been
    accomplished,
Until your strength disintegrates,
Until you too end
Not with a bang but in silence,
The way the trees go bare in November,
The way one finds a clock stopped.'

August 22, 1953

They Were a Hundred

They were a hundred men at arms.
When the sun rose in the sky,
They all took a step forward.
Hours passed, without a sound:
They didn't bat an eye.
When the bells rang,
All of them took a step ahead.
So the day went, it was evening,
But when the first star blossomed in the sky,
All at once, they took a step ahead.
'Get back, get away, foul ghosts:
Back to your old night.'
But no one answered; so, instead,
They took a step ahead, all in a ring.

March 1, 1959

Arrival*

Happy the man who's come to port,
Who leaves behind him seas and storms,
Whose dreams are dead or never born;
Who sits and drinks by the fire
At the beer hall in Bremen, and is at peace.
Happy the man like a flame gone out,
Happy the man like estuary sand,
Who has laid down his burden and wiped his
    brow
And rests by the side of the road.
He doesn't fear or hope or wait,
But stares intently at the setting sun.

September 10, 1964

* Cf. H. Heine, *Buch der Lieder,* 'Die Nordsee,' II, 9:
'*Glücklich der Mann, der den Hafen erreicht hat . . .*'

In the Beginning*

Fellow men for whom a year is long,
A century a venerable goal,
Exhausted earning your bread,
Worn out, enraged, deluded, sick, and lost;
Hear, and be consoled and mocked:
Twenty billion years ago,
Splendid, moving through both space and time,
There was a globe of flame, alone, eternal,
Our common father and our executioner,
And it exploded, and all change began.
Even now, the faint echo from this one catastro-
    phe reversal
Sounds from the far ends of the universe.
Everything was born from that one spasm:
The same abyss that embraces us and taunts us,
The same time that gives us life and ruins us,

* *'Bereshit,'* 'in the beginning,' is the first word of
Holy Scripture. On the big bang, to which allusion is
made, see for example *Scientific American*, June 1970.

Everything each of us has thought,
The eyes of every woman we have loved,
Suns by the thousand, too,
And this hand that writes.

August 13, 1970

The Dark Stars*

No one should sing again of love or war.

The order the cosmos took its name from has
    been dissolved;
The heavenly legions are a snarl of monsters,
The universe besieges us, blind, violent, and
    strange.
The sky is scattered with horrible dead suns,
Dense sediment of shattered atoms.
Only despairing heaviness emanates from them,
Not energy, not messages, not particles, not
    light;
Light itself falls back, broken by its own weight,
And all of us human seed we live and die for
    nothing,
And the heavens perpetually roil in vain.

November 30, 1974

* Cf. *Scientific American*, December 1974.

Farewell

It's grown late, dear ones;
So I won't take bread or wine from you
But only a few hours of silence,
The tales of the fisherman Peter,
The musky scent of this lake,
The ancient odor of burned shoots,
The screeching gossip of the gulls,
The free gold of the lichens on the roof tiles,
And a bed, to sleep alone in.
In return, I'll leave you nebbish* lines like these,
Made to be read by five or seven readers:
Then we'll go, each driven by his worries,
Since, as I was saying, it's grown late.

Anguillara, December 28, 1974

* 'Nebbish' is a Yiddish word. It means 'stupid,
useless, inept.'

The Girl of Pompeii

Since the anguish of each belongs to us all
We're still living yours, scrawny little girl
Clinging convulsively to your mother
As if you wanted to get back inside her
When the sky went black that afternoon.
To no avail, because the sky, turned poison,
Infiltrated the shut windows of your quiet
House with its thick walls to find you
Happy before in your song and timid laughter.
The centuries have passed, the ash has turned to
     stone,
Locking in these gentle limbs forever.
So you stay with us, contorted plaster cast,
Endless agony, horrific witness
To how our proud seed matters to the gods.
But there's nothing left for us of your far-away
     sister,
The girl from Holland walled up in four walls
Who wrote about her childhood without a
     tomorrow:

Her quiet ashes have been spread by the wind,
Her brief life held inside a crumpled notebook.
Nothing's left of the Hiroshima schoolgirl,
Shadow transfixed on the wall by the light of a
thousand suns,
Victim sacrificed on the altar of fear.
Masters of the earth lords of new poisons,
Sad secret guardians of definitive thunder,
The afflictions heaven offers us are sufficient.
Stop and consider before you push the button.

November 20, 1978

The Gulls of Settimo

Bend on bend, year after year,
The lords of the sky have come upriver,
Along the banks, up from its turbulent mouths.
They've forgotten backwash and salt water,
Shrewd, patient hunting, greedy crabs.
Above Crespino, Polesella, Ostiglia,
The newborns, more determined than the old,
Beyond Luzzara, beyond wasted Viadana,
Bloated with our ignoble
. Waste, fatter at every turn,
They've explored Caorso's mists,
The lazy tributaries between Cremona and
    Piacenza,
Borne on the tepid breath of the autostrada,
Shrieking their mournful, brief salute.
They've halted at the mouth of the Ticino,
Built nests under the bridge at Valenza,
Near mounds of tar and leftover polyethylene.
They've sailed to nowhere, beyond Casale and
    Chivasso,

Fleeing the sea, drawn on by our abundance.
Now they drift restless over Settimo Torinese:
Past forgotten, they pick over our waste.

April 9, 1979

To the Valley

The carriages trundle toward the valley,
Smoke from the brush hangs blue and bitter,
A bee, the last one, pointlessly noses the autumn
    crocuses;
Slow, waterlogged, the landslides shudder.
Mist rises quickly among the larches, as if called:
I've followed it in vain with my heavy, fleshy step,
Soon it will fall again as rain: the season's over,
Our half of the world wends toward winter.
And soon all our seasons will be over:
How long will these good limbs of mine
    obey me?
It's grown late to live and love,
To see into the sky and understand the world.
It's time to go down
To the valley, with shut, silent faces,
To shelter in the shadows of our troubles.

September 5, 1979

Heart of Wood

My next-door neighbor's sturdy:
A horse chestnut on Corso Re Umberto;
My age but he doesn't seem it,
He shelters sparrows and crows, and has no
    shame
Putting out buds and leaves in April,
Fragile flowers in May, and in September
Burrs with harmless spines
That hold shiny, tannic chestnuts.
An impostor, but naïve: he wants to seem
Like his fine mountain brother's rival,
Lord of sweet fruit and rare mushrooms.
It's not a happy life. The number 8
And 19 trams run across his roots
Every five minutes, leaving him deaf,
And he grows twisted, as if he wants to escape.
Year after year, he sucks up gentle poisons
From the methane-saturated subsoil;
He's drenched by dog piss,
The striations on his bark get clogged

With the avenues' polluted dust;
Under his bark hang desiccated
Chrysalises that will never be butterflies.
Still, in his slow-witted wooden heart
He senses and enjoys the changing seasons.

May 10, 1980

July 12, 1980

Be patient, my weary lady,
Patient with the things of this world,
With your fellow travelers, me included,
From the moment I was allotted to you.
After so many years, accept a few gnarled lines
For this important birthday.
Be patient, my impatient lady,
Pulverized and macerated, flayed,
Who flay yourself a little every day
So the raw flesh hurts you even more.
It's no longer time to live alone.
Please, accept these fourteen lines;
They're my rough way of telling you you're
    loved,
And that I wouldn't be in the world without you.

July 12, 1980

Autobiography

'Once I was both boy and girl, bush,
bird and silent fish jumping out of the sea.'

FROM A FRAGMENT BY EMPEDOCLES

I'm old like the world, I who speak to you.
In the dark of origins
I swarmed in the blind furrows of the sea,
Blind myself: but already I wanted the light
When I was still lying in the sea floor's filth.
I swilled salt with a thousand infinitesimal
    throats;
I was a fish, sleek and fast. I avoided traps,
I showed my young the sidewise tracks of the crab.
Taller than a tower, I offended the sky,
The mountains trembled at my storming step
And my brute hulk obstructed the valleys:
The rocks of your time still sport
The incredible mark of my scales.
I sang to the moon the liquid song of the toad,

And my patient hunger perforated wood.
Impetuous skittish stag
I ran through woods that are ashes today, and
gloried in my strength.
I was drunk cicada, astute horrendous tarantula,
And salamander and scorpion and unicorn and asp.
I suffered the whip
And heat and cold and the desperation of the yoke,
The donkey's silent vertigo at the millstone.
I was a girl, hesitant in the dance;
Geometer, I sought the secret of the circle
And the dubious ways of clouds and winds:
I knew tears and laughter and many loves.
Don't deride me, then, men of Agrigento,
If this old body is engraved with strange signs.

November 12, 1980

Voices*

Voices still forever, or since yesterday, or just now
    quieted;
If you cock your ear you can still catch their echo.
Hoarse voices of those who can speak no longer,
Voices that speak and no longer say a thing,
Voices that believe they're saying something,
Voices that speak and are not understood:
Choruses and cymbals to smuggle
A meaning into the message with no meaning,
Pure babble that pretends
That silence isn't silence.
À vous parle, compaings de galle:
I speak for you, raucous companions
Drunk like me on words:
Words-as-swords and words-as-poison
Key and picklock words,
Words of salt, mask and nepenthe.
The place we're going to is quiet

* Cf. F. Villon, *Le Testament*, 1. 1720.

Unfinished Business

Sir, please accept my resignation
As of next month,
And, if it seems right, plan on replacing me.
I'm leaving much unfinished work,
Whether out of laziness or actual problems.
I was supposed to tell someone something,
But I no longer know what and to whom: I've
    forgotten.
I was also supposed to donate something –
A wise word, a gift, a kiss;
I put it off from one day to the next. I'm sorry.
I'll do it in the short time that remains.
I'm afraid I've neglected important clients.
I was meant to visit
Distant cities, islands, desert lands;
You'll have to cut them from the program
Or entrust them to my successor.
I was supposed to plant trees and I didn't;
To build myself a house,
Maybe not beautiful, but based on plans.

Mainly, I had in mind
A marvelous book, kind sir,
Which would have revealed many secrets,
Alleviated pains and fears,
Eased doubts, given many
The gift of tears and laughter.
You'll find its outline in my drawer,
Down below, with the unfinished business;
I didn't have the time to write it out, which is a
    shame,
It would have been a fundamental work.

April 19, 1981

Passover*

Tell me: how is this night
Different from all other nights?
Tell me, how is this Passover
Different from other Passovers?
Light the light, unbar the door
So that the traveler may enter,
Be he Gentile or Jew:
Perhaps the prophet is hidden under his rags.
Enter and sit with us,
Listen, drink, and sing and celebrate Passover.
Eat the bread of affliction,
Lamb, sweet mortar, and bitter herbs.
This is the night of differences,
When we put our elbows on the table,
Because the forbidden is prescribed
So that evil may turn into good.
We'll spend the evening telling tales

* Contains various references to the traditional Jewish
ritual of Passover.

Of age-old wonderful events,
And because of all the wine
The hills will prance like rams.
Tonight the wise, the heathen, the fool, and the
    child
Ask each other questions,
And time changes direction,
Today flows back into yesterday,
Like a river silted up at its mouth.
Each of us has been a slave in Egypt,
Has soaked straw and clay with sweat
And crossed the sea with dry feet:
You, too, stranger.
This year in fear and shame,
Next year in strength and justice.

April 9, 1982

In Mothballs

Late and alone an old keel rocks,
Among the many new ones, in the slicked,
Oil-iridescent water of the harbor.
Its wood is leprous, its iron rusty orange.
Its hull knocks blind against the dock, obese
Like a belly pregnant with nothing.
Under the water's surface
You see soft seaweed, and the slow, slow drills
Of teredos and stubborn barnacles.
On the torrid deck, white splotches
Of calcined gull guano,
Tar oxidized by sun, and useless paint,
And brown stains, I'm afraid, of human
      excrement,
With spider lines of salt; I didn't know
Spiders too nested in mothballed ships.
I can't say what prey they're after, but they must
      know their work.
The tiller creaks and lazily obeys
The secret whims of all the little currents.

On the stern that saw the world,
A name and motto no longer legible.
But the mooring line is new,
Yellow and red nylon, taut and glossy,
Just in case the mad old dame
Had the wild idea of going to sea.

June 27, 1982

A Bridge

It's not like other bridges,
Which survive the snowfall of the centuries
So flocks can cross to water and pasture
Or revelers can go from place to place.
This is a different kind of bridge,
Happy if you stop halfway
And stare into the depths and ask yourself
If it's worthwhile to be alive tomorrow.
It's dull but alive
And never at rest.
Maybe because a poison slowly
Drips from its hollow pier,
An old maliciousness I won't describe;
Or maybe, as they said it late at night,
Because it's the product of a dirty deal.
Which is here why you never see the current
Tranquilly reflect the bridge's span,
But only cresting waves and eddies.

Which is why it's always scoured by sand,
Screaming, stone on stone,
And pushes pushes pushes against the banks
To break the earth's crust open.

November 25, 1982

Nachtwache*

'Watchman, what of the night?'

'I've heard the owl repeat
Its hollow warning note,
The bat shriek as it hunted,
the slither of the water snake
Under the pond's sodden leaves.
I've heard wine-soaked voices,
Garbled, angry, while I dozed,
From the bar next to the chapel.
I've heard lovers whispering,
The laughter and breathlessness of satisfied
    longing;
Adolescents murmuring in their sleep,
Others tossing sleepless with desire.
I've seen silent heat lightning,
I've seen the nightly terror

* 'Night watchman' in German (it was a technical
term in the Lager). The first line is from Isaiah 22:11.

Of the girl who's lost her mind
And can't tell bed from bier.
I've heard the raucous heaving
Of a lonely old man wrestling with death,
Of a woman torn in childbirth,
The wail of a newborn.
Lie down and sleep, citizen,
All is well: this night's half over.'

August 10, 1983

Flight*

Rock and sand and no water
Sand stitched with his footsteps
Numberless all the way to the horizon:
He was fleeing, though no one was chasing.
Crushed and scattered rubble
Stone eroded by wind
Split by frost after frost,
Dry wind and no water.
No water for him
Who needed only water,
Water to erase
Water savage dream
Impossible water to make him pure again.
Leaden rayless sun
Sky and dunes and no water
Ironic water made by mirages
Precious water poured off in sweat

* Cf. T. S. Eliot, *The Waste Land*, l. 332: 'Rock and no water and the sandy road.'

And up above the untapped water of the clouds.
    He found the well and went down,
He plunged his hands in and the water went red.
No one could ever drink it again.

January 12, 1984

The Survivor*

To B.V.

Since then, at an uncertain hour,
That agony returns:
And till his ghastly tale is told,
His heart within him burns.
He sees his comrades' faces
livid at first light,
gray with cement dust,
Vague in the mist,
Dyed by death in their restless sleep:
At night they grind their jaws
Under the heavy burden of their dreams
Chewing a nonexistent turnip.
'Back, away from here, drowned people,
Go. I haven't stolen anyone's place,
I haven't usurped the bread of anyone,

* Cf. S. T. Coleridge, *The Rime of the Ancient Mariner*,
l. 582, and *Inferno* XXXIII:141.

No one died for me. No one.
Go back to your haze.
It's not my fault if I live and breathe
And eat and drink and sleep and put on clothes.'

February 4, 1984

Sidereus Nuncius

I've seen two-horned Venus
Navigating suavely in the sky.
I've seen valleys and mountains on the Moon
And three-bodied Saturn,
I, Galileo, first among humans;
Four stars orbiting Jupiter,
And the Milky Way disintegrating
Into infinite legions of new worlds.
I've seen, though I did not believe, ominous spots
Infecting the face of the Sun.
I built this telescope myself,
A learned man but with wise hands:
I polished its mirrors, I aimed it at the Sky
The way you'd aim a bombard.
I was the one who broke Heaven open
Before the Sun burned my eyes.

 Before the Sun burned my eyes
 I had to bend and say
 I didn't see what I saw.
 He who chained me to the earth

Didn't loose earthquakes or lightning,
   He had a low, flat voice,
He had a face like everyman.
The vulture that gnaws at me every evening
Has the face of everyman.

April 11, 1984

Give Us

Give us something to destroy,
A crown, a quiet place,
A trusted friend, a magistrate,
A phone booth,
A journalist, a renegade,
A fan of the opposing team,
A lamppost, a manhole cover, a bench.
Give us something to deface,
A plaster wall, the Mona Lisa,
A mudguard, a gravestone,
Give us something to defile,
A timid girl,
A flower bed, ourselves.
Don't despise us, we are heralds and prophets.
Give us something that burns, offends, cuts,
    breaks, befouls,
That makes us feel we exist.
Give us a club or a Nagant,
Give us a syringe or a Suzuki.
Pity us.

April 30, 1984

Dust

How much dust
Lies on the nervous tissue of a life?
Dust has no weight or sound,
No color or intention: it obscures, denies,
Obliterates, hides, paralyzes;
It doesn't kill, it smothers.
It isn't dead. It sleeps.
It harbors spores millennia old
Pregnant with future damage,
Tiny chrysalises waiting
To break up, decompose, degrade:
Pure mixed-up indefinite ambush
Ready for the assault to come,
Powerlessness that will be power
At the sounding of a silent signal.
But it also harbors different germs,
Dormant seeds that will become ideas,
Each one instinct with a universe
Unforeseen, new, beautiful, and strange.
Therefore respect and fear

This gray and shapeless mantle:
It holds evil, good,
Danger, and many written things.

September 29, 1984

Still to Do

I wouldn't disturb the universe.
I'd like, if possible,
To get free silently,
Light-footed, like a smuggler,
The way one slips away from a party.
To halt the stubborn pumping of my lungs
Without a squeal,
And tell my lovely heart,
That mediocre musician with no rhythm:
'After 2.6 billion heartbeats
You must be tired, too; thank you, it's enough.'
If possible, as I was saying –
If it weren't for those who stay behind,
For the work cut short
(Each life's cut short),
For the world's turns and wounds;
it wasn't for the unfinished business,
The long-standing debts,
The old unavoidable commitments.

December 10, 1984

Airport

It was a sampling of man in transit,
As if selected at random
For inspection by an alien buyer:
Rich and poor and fat and slim,
Indians, blacks, the sick, and children.
What does man in transit do?
Nothing of significance.
Chats and sleeps and smokes in his seat:
What will the buyer say? What will he offer
For that seventy-year-old woman in tights?
For that group of eight talking nonsense,
Grandparents, mothers, grand- and
    great-grandchildren?
For that family of fatties
Stuck in their chair?
For the two of us, fed up with foreign words?

We're leaving. The great cavelike bird
Sucks up everyone indiscriminately:
We cross Acheron

Via a telescopic concourse.
It taxis, accelerates, gathers power,
Lifts off, and suddenly is raised into the sky
Body and soul: our bodies and souls.
Are we worthy of Assumption?

Now it flies into the purple twilight
Over the ice of nameless seas,
Or above a mantle of dark clouds,
As if this planet of ours
Had hidden its face in shame.
Now it's flying with dull thuds
Almost as if someone were driving piles
Into the Stygian swamp;
Now along soft,
Smoothed tracks of air.
The night is without sleep, but brief,
Brief the way no night has ever been:
Light and carefree like a first night.

At Malpensa, Lisa with her bright,
alert expression was expecting us.
I don't think it was a useless trip.

May 29, 1985